First English edition published by Colour Library Books Ltd.
© 1984 Illustrations and text: Colour Library Books Ltd.,
    Guildford, Surrey, England.
This edition published by Crescent Books.
Distributed by Crown Publishers, Inc.
hgfedcba
Display and text filmsetting by Acesetters Ltd.,
    Richmond, Surrey, England.
Colour separations by Llovet S.A., Barcelona, Spain.
Printed and bound in Barcelona, Spain by Rieusset and Gráficas Estella.
ISBN 0 517 462761
CRESCENT 1984

MICHAEL JACKSON
The Victory Tour

DAVID LEVENSON

Produced by

Ted Smart

and

Gerald Hughes

Edited by

David Gibbon

Designed by

Philip Clucas MSIAD

CRESCENT BOOKS
NEW YORK

Victory is the name of their tour. Victory is the name of their album. And victory was in the air from the moment the lights first dimmed on the Kansas stage which brought the Jacksons back to the ecstatic public. Perhaps it's too early to talk of victory when the gladiators are only in their twenties, but you knew from that first orchestration of screaming – intense, spontaneous, embracing – that there would be no talk of defeat or dissolution this year.

For two years, Michael Jackson and his brothers – you prayed for their reunion, and here it is at last – meticulously planned this mind-blowing, one hundred million dollar bonanza, designed to spread the dramatic, unrepeatable experience of space-age spectacle and voodoo thrills through no fewer than thirteen major American cities. Los Angeles to New York. Detroit to Dallas. Jacksonville, of course. It all began right in the middle of the republic, when Kansas City saw its previous concert

crowd records blown sky-high by the one hundred and thirty-five thousand who packed the Arrowhead Stadium for those three unforgettable July nights. Instantly, Elvis, the Beatles and the Rolling Stones became as historical as King Arthur.

It's the stuff dreams are made of, but even the wildest dream is upstaged by the Jackson Victory extravaganza. Imagine a darkening, sultry evening, electric with blazing artificial light and with the tension of anticipation as tens of thousands of rock-hungry fans await the explosion and brilliance of noise and vision, the sight and sound of the god-like miracle boy-king of pop, his vulnerably waif-thin figure and unruly kiss-curl marking him out from his elder, sturdier brothers. With every passing second the atmosphere becomes increasingly unbearable; minutes seem like years; a momentary fidget erupts into unstoppable leaping; whimpers of excitement amplify into screams of frustration. The agony of impatience is

deliberately prolonged way past the scheduled witching hour, the prospective emotional ugliness eventually avoided with impeccable timing by the sudden sensation of lights going out all around. Within seconds the place is enveloped in darkness. For almost five minutes there is nothing to see, yet the cheering echoes like thunder through the night sky. Everyone knows something will happen – a hope fulfilled, a promise kept – yet no one knows what, how, or even when.

Nor can you possibly have imagined it. In place of the expected brothers, five monsters boom onto a massive black stage, their presence lit in five different colors by the first of the night's great laser successes. These are no agile young pop heroes, but menacing Star Wars figures whose stamping progress is made more sinister by the rhythmic bang of unseen drums and clashing metal. The message of planet Earth once dominated by fiery-eyed creatures of evil is immediately clear – candle-clutching

Kreetons plodding inexorably to their own destruction. Now you begin to understand. Here in the middle of the stage rises an enormous, glowing stone, and in it a sword pulsating with light. A glittering human form advances, attempts to extract the weapon, and fails. A second shining knight wrenches the sword from its stone sheath, and flicks its point toward his awed spectators. They have already begun to cheer and when he announces, "Arise, behold the kingdom," there is pandemonium as the sword expels darting laser beams which shower them in a red and green confetti of brilliance. You cannot help believing that the Earth has just been liberated; the relief is all around you; the response deafening as the triumphant knight battles to end the monsters' threats forever.

Yet all this is as nothing to the reaction when a bank of lights, space-ship bright, rises from the stage floor to reveal five slim silhouettes striding towards its edge, an insistent pounding of drums

accompanying each synchronized footstep. You and all around you have leapt onto chairs, waving arms, yelling, even weeping in an ecstasy of almost frightening power. The brothers erupt at last into their first number. *Wanna Be Startin' Something* booms out. Michael, that sometimes elusive, secretive, even faintly bizarre pagan deity, is where he belongs – center stage, clenching that famous, white-gloved fist in salute to his worshippers. Halfway through, the frilled glove – his glittering, rhinestone-studded hallmark, a symbol of unity and even faith kept with loyal followers – is teasingly removed, to allow concentration upon the succession of superb outfits Michael and his brothers have chosen for this colossal, inter-city Victory tour.

At first the human quintet appears as a symphony in black and white. Foremost among them Michael, in black and white striped pants and a short white jacket layered with sparkling rhinestones. Soon the jacket is whipped off, unexpectedly and to the frenzied delight of thousands

of young girls, to reveal a virginal white sequined shirt beneath a wide, frilled sash. Its purity contrasts with the gaudy, shocking pink space suit he will wear for a later theatrical spasm, and with some of his brothers' more extreme tastes. Randy, for instance, chooses to wear silver sequined shin guards; Tito asserts his independence with a red-trimmed baseball uniform sporting his name emblazoned in a blue frost across the chest.

Mundane shin guards and baseball caps only serve to enhance the weird, magical drama of this unique spectacular. Just about every major song the Jacksons have stunned the Western world with is here and now. The incomparable *Billie Jean* lives again, moody as never before; its final chords stressed by the nonchalant tossing away of Michael's fedora. Here too, exquisitely contrasted, are *Beat It, Human Nature, Rock With You* and *Lovely One*. And Michael's darker, more personal side is tantalizingly exposed in his emotional

rendering of *Heartbreak Hotel* and, of course, *She's Out Of My Life.* If you have tears, and you will have, prepare to shed them here. This love story is so heavy with physical emotion that it has a thousand girls weeping in the aisles as Michael himself, breathless and choking on his words, dabs away the tears.

It has its lighter side of course – there is something for everyone. The horseplay with Jermaine is significant as well as entertaining, for it acknowledges the compromises the brothers have made for this, their great reunion. Jermaine gets a 12-minute solo spell, trying out three of his latest songs. He wants to continue, but his brothers' return won't let him. Marlon suggests to Tito that they stick to old favorites. Tito agrees. Jermaine protests. Good-humored banter takes over before the golden oldies inevitably strike up. The audience has no doubt what it wants. The cheers and renewed applause for *I Want You Back, The Love You Save* and *I'll Be There* are proof that

the Jacksons are here to sta believes Randy's claim abou amazing talent. No one beli Michael may never join his again while a tour like this such instant, complete succ

The statistics will stun you. is no forced term when two pounds of dry ice provide b smoke effects for each show almost three thousand gallo cool the lasers as their mul zag searches out an audienc gesticulating limbs and exci Special effect technicians c around on a five-story stage seventeen operators track th which suffuse the arena, ba performers and blind the pa stadiums. Two dozen articu ferry almost four hundred t equipment from big city to Rehearsals, begun in Febru of five hours a day, six days eventually consume an eigh

to satisfy Michael's obsessive quest for perfection. These enormities are reflected in the gigantic scenarios that will live with you for a lifetime. The massive, menacing spider of light which descends onto the stage, enclosing its victims, pincer-style, in legs of ever changing colors; the illusion of Michael's disappearance in a swirl of fabric, confounded by his reappearance atop a huge structure of white pillars; the even more personal illusion of Michael's celebrated "moon walking", rehearsed and polished to the ultimate in finesse. And the fireworks. As a finale there is a succession of lighting tricks which never fail to amaze and thrill, the last burst of lasers shooting out from stage to

audience are attended by a monumental, megawatt explosion of fireworks. Glorious, pulsating, whirling, fizzing, soaring pyrotechnics are sustained by musical noise and the incessant wild whoops and cheers of captivated witnesses. You would never think they have just heard Michael tell them, "That's the end, I love you all."

No wonder the organizers announced that the concert would be played virtually unchanged throughout the entire tour of 49 performances. It has success stamped all over it, and the hundreds of thousands of fans who have seen or have booked to see it are living proof of that. Michael Jackson lookalikes mushroom everywhere – dark glasses, white gloves and glittering gear proclaiming their devotion. But behind them are armies of less obvious, yet equally dedicated followers whose dream of the reunited Jacksons has been realized – in Victory.